I0785743

The Dove: An Example of Attachment to Home

by New York General Protestant Episocal

with an introduction by Jackson Chambers

This work contains material that was originally published in 1849.

This publication is within the Public Domain.

*This edition is reprinted for educational purposes
and in accordance with all applicable Federal Laws.*

The World's Largest Selection of Vintage Poultry Books

www.VintagePoultry.com

Self Reliance Books

Get more historic titles on animal and stock breeding, gardening and old fashioned skills by visiting us at:

http://selfreliancebooks.blogspot.com/

Introduction

I am pleased to present yet another historic title on raising Pigeons.

        The work is in the Public Domain and is re-printed here in accordance with Federal Laws.

        As with all reprinted books of this age that are intended to perfectly reproduce the original edition, considerable pains and effort had to be undertaken to correct fading and sometimes outright damage to existing proofs of this title. At times, this task is quite monumental, requiring an almost total "rebuilding" of some pages from digital proofs of multiple copies. Despite this, imperfections still sometimes exist in the final proof and may detract from the visual appearance of the text. The original plates in these titles are often moved to the rear of the text to adhere to modern publication standards.

        I hope you enjoy reading this book as much as I enjoyed making it available to readers again.

Jackson Chambers

THE DOVE,

THE dove let loose in Eastern skies,
  Returning fondly home,
Ne'er stoops to earth her wing, nor flies
  Where idler warblers roam.

But high she shoots, through air and light,
  Above all low decay,
Where nothing earthly bounds her flight,
  Nor shadow dims her way.

So grant me, Lord, from every snare
  Of sinful passion free,
Aloft through virtue's purer air,
  To steer my course to thee.

No sin to cloud, no lure to stay
  My soul, as home she springs ;
Thy sunshine on her joyful way,
  Thy freedom on her wings.

THE love of home is one of the strongest emotions of the human mind, and appears to have been implanted within us
for the wisest and best ends.   Home is,
to most of us, the centre of our affections,
and the place where our chief earthly
treasure is to be found.   Whether rich or
poor, young or old, we all naturally feel
a strong interest in everything relating to
home ; nor is that interest lost, when
poverty or misfortune has stripped us of
many comforts, and has left of home
little more than the name.   In childhood,
home is the place where protection and
sympathy are always to be found, where
parental love is ready to soothe our sor-
rows and our fears, and where all our

wants and wishes may be freely poured out, and are sure to meet with ready attention. In more advanced years, to have a home of our own is the great object of ambition, and when attained, there is not only the feeling of affection for those who are associated with us in it, but there is likewise the sense of our own right and property in it, which makes it dear and pleasant to our eyes.

The love of home operates beneficially on the character. The examples and precepts of a good home are constantly before the eyes, and acting on the conduct of a right-minded youth. To win the approbation of those at home, is a sufficient motive for exertion, and to go back to them with the prospect of meeting their just and willing praises, is the dearest object of hope. A religious and well-ordered home affords, indeed, the nearest approach to a state of perfect happiness, which this earth can present, and may be considered, without presumption, as a feeble type of the bliss of that Heavenly Home, where the Lord has promised to provide " a place " for those who love Him.

It is true, that there are some perverse and disorderly spirits, which can set at nought the counsels of parents, and despise all the sweet ties of home; while there are many more who are so unhappy as to have an evil instead of a good example set them at home, and have therefore no reason to love it. These are deplorable cases, and most difficult to be dealt with. Each one of us may, however, contribute his own share to the general well-being of society by faithfully fulfilling the duties, and thoroughly valuing the privileges of home.

Many of the lower animals, even in their state of dependence or captivity to man, are found reading him a lesson on the love of home. Who has not heard extraordinary stories of the fondness of the cat for the place where she has been brought up, and of the distance she will travel to reach it, finding her way with the greatest certainty, although she may have been conveyed away in a close basket, or sack, and could not have made any observations on the road. Similar things might be told of the dog, though in his case, the affection seems rather towards the person of his master, than to the place of his abode. Sheep have been known to return from a great distance to their old pastures; and even the ass, to whom we usually attribute a large share of stupidity, has been cunning enough to traverse a distance of two hundred miles, through an unknown and mountainous country, until he reached the stable where he had been formerly kept.

But, perhaps, the most remarkable proof of attachment to home, is that afforded by the various species of dove, especially the carrier dove, or pigeon.—This bird is well known to possess the most wonderful faculty of discovering its own abode, and returning to it, when carried to a very great distance. This power is connected with that strong affection for its mate and home, which the bird ever displays.

From the earliest ages, doves have been regarded as the emblems of gentleness and innocence. Their beautiful plumage, their tender voices, and their loving nature, have attracted the notice of mankind, and especially of poets, who have duly celebrated the praises of these affectionate birds. The dove is also frequently mentioned in Holy Writ. The dove was the messenger sent forth from the ark, to ascertain whether the water had subsided from the earth, and returning with an olive branch in her mouth, she became thenceforth the emblem of peace. "A pair of turtle-doves, or two young pigeons," were accepted as an offering to the Lord, under the Mosaic dispensation. The beautiful plumage of the dove supplied the Psalmist with the simile in which it is said of the righteous, "they shall be as the wings of a dove covered with silver, and her feathers with yellow gold." The rapid flight of the dove is also alluded to in the pathetic Psalm, where he says, "Oh, that I had wings like a dove! then would I flee away and be at rest." (Ps. lv. 6.) The tender voice of doves is noticed by the prophet

Isaiah, when he represents the suffering Jews as mourning "sore like doves."— The gentleness of disposition for which these birds are remarkable, and the innocence and simplicity of their nature were not unmarked by our Saviour, who cautioned his disciples, when in the midst of enemies, to be "wise as serpents, and harmless as doves." (Matt. x. 16.) Finally, the highest honour was bestowed on the dove when it was made the type of the Holy Spirit of God, and thus became the emblem of all that was pure, peaceful, and holy.

The different species of dove known in this country* are four in number, and all have nearly the same characteristics.— The colors of the plumage are softly blended, so as to produce a uniform tint, except in the wing and tail feathers,

* England.

which are mixed with black. The attachment of the bird for its mate appears to last for life, and is shown by continual marks of fondness, and the tenderest notes of affection. But if the death of one of the pair leaves the other alone, the survivor does not pine away in fruitless sorrow for its mate, as is sometimes affirmed, but, when the season comes round, he chooses another mate, and rears his young as before. In confinement, the case is different; when shut up in a cage a pair of these gentle birds may thrive for a time, but if one dies, the other generally sickens, which has perhaps given rise to the above opinion.

The cooing of doves is a plaintive and expressive sound, which harmonises well with the subdued murmurings of brooks, and sighing of breezes in the quiet and secluded spots which these birds frequent.

> Deep in the wood, thy voice I list, and love
> Thy soft complaining song—thy tender cooing ;
> O, what a winning way thou hast of wooing !
> Gentlest of all thy race—sweet Turtle-dove.

The wild pigeons of this country are the *ring-dove*, the *turtle-dove*, the *stock-dove*, and the *rock-dove*. The first is the largest, the best known, and the most ornamental of the four. It has many common provincial names, such as the wood-pigeon, the cushat, the quest, &c. It is a graceful and beautiful bird, with plumage of peculiar changing grey on the head and neck, deepening to a purplish tint on the back, and becoming purplish red on the under parts, with greenish reflections. On the neck are two spots of white, one on each side. These nearly meet behind, forming a collar or ring, which has given the name to the bird. Its plaintive song begins in February, and may often be heard in pine plantations, where the ring-dove likes to make its home. The building time is early in April, and although the bird is generally shy and retired in its habits, yet it sometimes builds in pleasure grounds close to houses, and becomes fa-

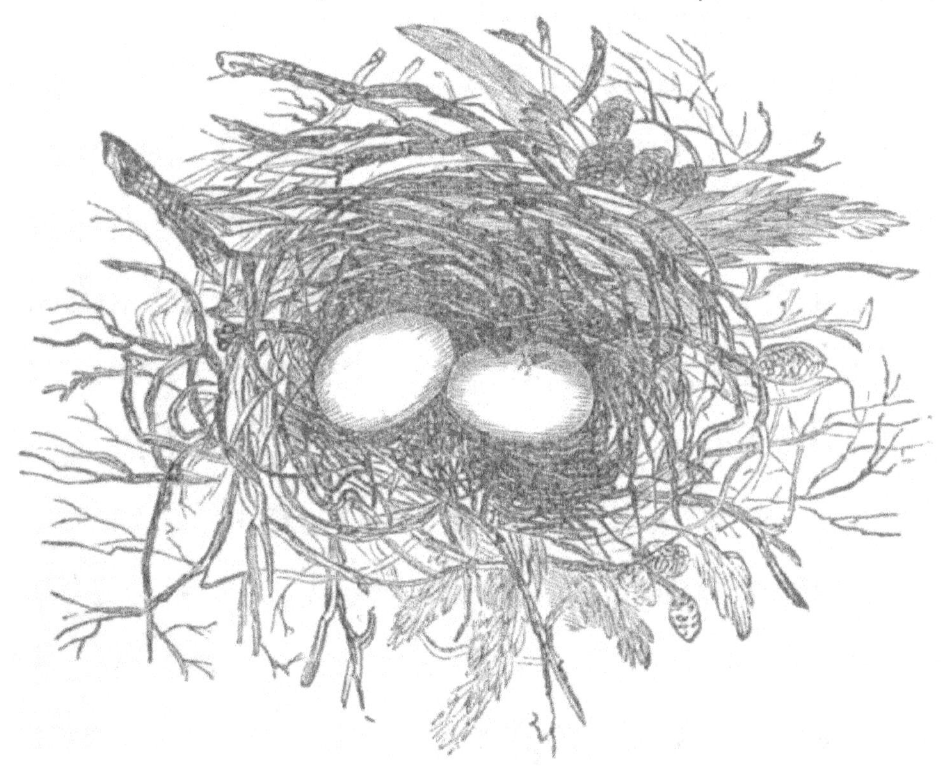

NEST OF THE RING-DOVE.

miliarized to the noises of such situations. A ring-dove's nest has been seen in a bush near which children have been playing all day long; and a case has been known of these birds building and rearing young in the ivy immediately beneath a window. But this is a most unusual occurrence. The nest is very slightly made, being nothing more than a few twigs, laid so carelessly together that the eggs may sometimes be seen from below. The eggs are only two in number, which is the case with all the other doves. The broods are often three in the year. Seeds and other vegetable substances are the chief food of these birds, and these are prepared in the craw, or crop, before they pass into the true stomach. The food of most birds, when of a kind to require preparation, is moistened and separated in this manner, but in the doves there is a remarkable change in the crop of both the parent birds when feeding their young. " At that time the inner coat becomes covered with small glands, which secrete a peculiar fluid, which acquires a consistency resembling that of soft curd. When the young first break the shell, they are fed upon that substance, wholly or nearly, in a pure state; but, as they grow, it gradually mingles with more and more of the food of the parent bird, which it reduces to a sort of pulp; and when the young are able to feed themselves, the secretion disappears, and the glands that produced it are inactive until they are again required for the feeding of another progeny." The feeding of the young is performed by the parent putting its bill, half-opened, fairly into that of the little one, and thus delivering the curd or more solid food which is in readiness for it.

The stock-dove is smaller than the ring-dove, and is not often seen, except in the midland counties. It received its name from the supposition (an erroneous one) that it was the *stock* from whence our common pigeon was derived. The habits of the birds, are, however, very different. The stock-dove always nestles in trees or tall bushes, while the pigeon, instead of perching on branches, prefers to resort to holes, or pigeon-houses. The colour and make of the birds also present several points of difference. The stock-dove is a settled inhabitant in our island, but there are also many visitants of this species which arrive in winter from the north of Europe, and leave us again in the spring.

The rock-dove, which nestles in high cliffs on the sea-shore, appears to be the real " stock " from which our domestic pigeon comes. It perches, not on trees, but on ledges and points of rock, and if a pigeon-house be built very near the spot, the rock-doves will take possession of it, especially if it be white-washed. The females hatch from three to twelve broods in a year, and for the production of the shells of so many eggs they require a great deal of carbonate of lime. The whitened pigeon-house is, therefore, very attractive to them, and they eagerly consume the lime of the white-wash. From the same necessity it is supposed that they keep near the shore, where the shells on the beach supply them abundantly with lime. On the rocky parts of the West of Scotland, especially on the bold shores of the Hebrides, these birds abound to an extent not known in any other part of the kingdom. They are fond of nestling in caves and holes of the rock, and frequently congregate in great numbers in one large cavern. This circumstance is taken advantage of by boatmen, as they are showing the caves to visitors, to produce a startling effect. Their plan is thus described by a Scottish writer:—" They row into the caves as silently as possible, until they have advanced some little way; then the steersman seizes a fowling-piece, which has been stowed away, and the rowers cease pulling. In an instant, and before the passengers have time to inquire what is the matter, the musket is discharged, the rowers thunder on the gunwale with their oars, and out dash the pigeons in a torrent-flood, making so loud a rustling and rumbling with their wings, that those to whom it is a novelty can hardly persuade themselves that the whole materials of the cave are not hurling down, in order to entomb them in a majestic sepulchre. But the din, though loud and not unalarming, does not last long, as the pigeons are fully as much affrighted as the passengers; and, as far as the roof of

the cavern can be seen, it is as stable as
ever, and not an ounce of stone is loos-
ened from its place. Fingal's Cave, in
the wild and beautifully green Isle of
Staffa, which isle is perforated through
and through under the low-water mark,
and absolutely rocks, like an unstable
thing, before the swell of the Atlantic,
when the majesty of that ocean is up,
used to be, if it is not still, a favourite
place for this kind of exhibition. The
cave is large and lofty, and if the interior
of it is not absolutely dark, it is dim twi-
light, and, as much of the roof consists of
portions of basaltic columns, hanging, as
it were, by simple contact with each
other, there are few roofs of caverns, the
fall of which would be more likely to be
expected by one who does not under-
stand the firm texture and stable union of
this wonderful architecture of nature.—

Another thing, basalt is perhaps the most sonorous of all rocks, and therefore the echoes of the cave itself go to swell the sound made by the numerous wings of its inhabitants. When the birds are thus disturbed, it is generally in the time of their repose; and hence, after they have escaped from the cave, they fly no farther than they may apprehend that the danger is to follow them."

The turtle-dove is the smallest of the four species known in Britain. It is a summer visitor to the south-eastern parts of our island, arriving in April or May, and keeping much to the shade of the close coppices, where it forms its nest. This bird is oftener heard than seen, being more shy and timid than any of the other doves, yet more easily tamed than they. If a pair is caught, the attachment of the birds for each other continues; they also caress the hand that feeds them, and their whole manners are remarkably simple and graceful. Yet small and gentle as they are, these birds, in their wild state, sometimes commit pretty extensive havoc on the fields of peas. As soon as the peas are formed in the pods, the turtles come more abroad, being attracted by this, their favorite food. The county of Kent forms the head-quarters for these birds, and when the time of migration approaches, they are seen collecting in little flocks on Romney Marsh, and other open places near the south-eastern shore. In England, the turtle has no time to rear a second brood, for in the month of August it generally quits our shores, although, in very mild seasons, it is said to linger through the winter, and sometimes to survive it. The turtle-dove makes a very rude nest, and deposits in it two white eggs, which are more pointed than those of the other species.

All these birds are remarkable for their gentle disposition and plaintive notes; but it is in some of the foreign species of dove that we have the most extraordinary instances of those journeys through the air, which have excited so much astonishment. The carrier pigeon, originally from the East, has been renowned for ages for the wonderful instinct and great powers of flight which enable it to return from great distances to its breeding place. The love of home is the powerful principle which urges its rapid flight; but in what way it discovers the direction it must take to reach the desired spot, is a mystery.— The instinct of these birds has been turned to account among mankind from an early period, and their importance as letter-carriers is well known. The way in which this is managed, is as follows: supposing two merchants, one residing in Brussels, the other in London, wished to communicate with each other by means of these birds, they must form their plans accordingly : the Brussels merchant would send a number of full grown carrier-pigeons reared by himself, to London, and the London merchant would send an equal number of his own rearing to Brussels. Thus each merchant would be in possession of a number of captive pigeons, eager to return to their homes ; and when an important message required to be speedily conveyed from the one place to the other, it would only be necessary to fasten a letter beneath the wing of one of the pigeons, and set it at liberty. With a perception altogether wonderful and unaccountable, the bird speeds its way to its former home, and appears in the old familiar dove-cot with the letter attached to its wings.

Mention is made of these winged letter-carriers by the ancient classic writers, and by the Arabian poets. By this means victories were announced, and communication was carried on with besieged cities. "Of what use," says Pliny, "were sentinels, circumvallation, or nets obstructing the rivers, when intelligence could be conveyed by aerial messengers?" But in later times the cunning of man converted this practice into one of doubt and danger, and it fell into disuse. During the time of the crusades, at the siege of Tyre, pigeons were observed hovering over the city, and being suspected to be carriers, one of them was captured by the besieging army, and laden with false intelligence. The poor bird conveyed its message, and thus became the means of the city's downfall.

A regular system of posting was once established in the East by means of carrier-pigeons. Lofty towers were erected by the Turkish government at the distance of thirty miles apart, and each of these was provided with a due supply of pigeons under the management of sentinels, whose business it was to receive the winged messengers and transmit the intelligence they brought by others. The message or letter was written on 'a very thin slip of paper, and inclosed in a small gold box, almost as thin as the paper itself, which was fastened to the neck of the bird. The hour of arrival and departure was marked at each tower, and for greater security, a duplicate was always dispatched two hours after the first. This regular system of posting no longer exists in Turkey, but carrier-pigeons are still much used there. The author of a treatise on Domestic Pigeons informs us, that " the Turks made a common practice of breeding the carrier-pigeons in their seraglios, where there is one whose business it is to feed and train these birds for the use afterwards designed—which is done in this manner :—When a young one flies very hard at home, and is come to its full strength, they carry it in a basket or otherwise about half a mile from home, and there turn it out: after this, they carry it a mile, then two, four, eight, ten, twenty, &c., till at length it will return from the farthest parts of the kingdom. This practice is of admirable use, for every bashaw has generally a basket full of these pigeons sent him from the grand seraglio; and in case of any insurrection, or other emergent occasion, he braces a letter under the wings of a pigeon, whereby its flight is not the least incommoded, and immediately turns it loose ; but for fear of its being shot, or struck by a hawk, he generally dispatches five or six ; so that by this means tidings are sent in a more safe and speedy method than could possibly be otherwise contrived. The paper on which these messages are written, is of peculiar fineness, and being employed only for this use, is called " bird-paper."

When the Turkey Company of England was in the height of its prosperity, and a number of English merchants were settled at Aleppo, they employed carrier-pigeons to bring them the earliest intelligence from the port of Scanderoon, which was nearly three days journey from Aleppo by any ordinary conveyance, but which the pigeons traversed in about three hours. Thus those merchants who employed pigeons, were in possession of important intelligence within three hours of the arrival of ships at the port, and long before the rest of the citizens had any tidings. On one occasion, a merchant killed one of these pigeons by accident, and learned from the billet under its wing, that there was a great scarcity of galls in England. Taking advantage of this, and buying up nearly the whole quantity in the market, he at once cleared a sum which was in those days considered an ample fortune.

At no very distant period, carrier-pigeons were employed in our own metropolis, to convey tidings of the execution or respite of criminals. In those days, executions were much more numerous than at present, often including persons among the upper classes, and the gallows at Tyburn was in constant use. There were also frequent instances of persons being sentenced, and dragged from Newgate to Tyburn, and after all, escaping with a longer or shorter imprisonment. The chance of pardon or respite at the foot of the gallows, kept the friends of criminals in suspense until the last moment; and when these were persons of some consideration, they caused carrier-pigeons to be conveyed to Tyburn, and dismissed the moment the result was known, thus conveying the intelligence with great rapidity to distant friends of the criminal.

Carrier-Pigeons are still employed as messengers between the chief cities of Europe, to convey important commercial intelligence; but their use is in some degree superseded by the power of steam, which enables us to travel at a speed nearly equalling the flight of the bird.

Two inferior varieties of the carrier-pigeon, known as the " dragoon" and the " horseman," have been cultivated in England, chiefly to gratify curiosity, and as a department of sport. A gentleman, in London, once sent a dragoon by the stage-coach to his friend at St. Edmund's-bury, with a request that two days after its arrival it might be thrown up precisely when the town clock struck nine in the morning. This was done, and the pigeon arrived at its home in London, which was a loft in the Bull Inn, Bishopsgate-street, at half-past eleven o'clock the same morning, having flown seventy-two miles in two hours and a half.

In July, 1819, an experiment, on which large sums of money depended, was made with carrier-pigeons between London and Antwerp. Thirty-two pigeons, with the word "Antwerp" marked on their wings, and which had been reared in that city, were let loose in our metropolis at seven o'clock in the morning, after having their wings counter-marked with the name of "London;" the same day, towards noon, one of these pigeons arrived at its home in Antwerp, and obtained the first prize; a quarter of an hour afterwards another arrived, and gained the second prize. The following day twelve others arrived; but of the fate of the rest no account is given.

In July, 1829, another experiment was made between Maestricht and London. Forty-two pigeons were brought to our metropolis, and after being properly marked, were thrown up at twenty-six minutes past eight in the morning. If any one of the number had reached Maestricht within six hours, the principal wager, which was for ten thousand guilders, would have been gained; but in consequence, as it was supposed, of heavy rain, the first did not arrive till six hours and a quarter from the time when it left London, having, nevertheless, travelled at the rate of forty-five miles an hour. Four days had elapsed before the greater number of the pigeons had arrived. In both these experiments there were many pigeons who had lost their way, or at least were never heard of more, and this shows the necessity for a precaution which is always employed when any very important message is to be transmitted by these winged carriers,—namely, that of dispatching two or three birds at the same time, each bearing the same message.

Thus has the truth and faithfulness of the dove to its early home, caused it to serve the purposes of mankind for centuries. And lest the mere love of its resting-place should be insufficient, man has added other means to make it a faithful messenger. A male and female are generally kept together, and treated well, and one of these, when taken elsewhere, is supposed to have the greater inducement to go back. Where great importance is attached to the message, it is sometimes sent by a female pigeon, who was taken away, either from her eggs or half-fledged young. But this trial of the poor bird's affection is probably unnecessary; for there is no reason to doubt, unless accident befel her, that she would faithfully return to her home without these additional inducements.

The carrier is larger than the common pigeon, being about fifteen inches long from the bill to the tail, and weighing about twenty ounces. It is generally black or dun; though sometimes blue or mottled with blue. It has a fleshy appendage hanging down on each side of its bill, like that of the male turkey. This appendage is very large, and consists of naked skin, of a whitish colour, hanging down as a sort of wattle, and extending forwards until it terminates in a point about the middle of the length of the bill. The amateurs of carrier-pigeons estimate their goodness by the wattle. Whether rightly or not, they consider those pigeons the best whose wattles rise high on the head, and have the portion round the eyes very broad. The dealers in these birds, therefore, endeavour to increase the apparent size of the wattle, and in some cases contrive to insert a piece of cork below the hind part, fastening it with a bit of wire. This practice is cruel, and injurious to the bird.

On being released the carrier rises to a great height, makes two or three circles in the air, and then commences its forward career. Some naturalists think that this circular flight is continued until the keen sight of the bird can recognize some known object. Rennie says, "We have not a doubt it is by the eye alone that the carrier-pigeon performs those extraordinary aerial journeys, which have, from the earliest ages, excited astonishment. We have frequently witnessed the experiment made with other pigeons, of taking them to a distance from the dove-cot, expressly to observe their manner of finding their way back, and we feel satisfied that their proceedings are uniformly the same. On being let go from the bag, in which they have been carried to conceal from their notice the objects on the road, they dart off on an irregular excursion, as if it were more to ascertain the reality of their freedom than to make an effort to return.

When they find themselves at full liberty, they direct their flight in circles round the spot whence they have been liberated, not only increasing the diameter of the circle, but rising at the same time gradually higher. This is continued as long as the eye can discern the bird, and hence we conclude, that it is also continued after we lose sight of them, a constantly-increasing circle being made till they ascertain some known object, enabling them to shape a direct course."

This may, perhaps, be the true mode of accounting for the bird's return from a distance of some few miles; for, supposing it to make a very wide circle in the air, it would probably see some familiar object, at one part of the circle or the other, and thus have a guide to its career; but when the distance is so great as from London to Brussels, or some other continental town, it is impossible to explain the bird's proceedings in the same way. Carrier-pigeons generally cross the channel in safety, and reach their homes in a very short space of time. It is only in misty or foggy weather that there is any danger of the birds losing their way, and being lost; and although this proves that they are, to a certain extent, guided by sight, yet it cannot be supposed that sight alone is the power which enables them to perform those long and astonishing journeys.

The longing after home, which is evidently the spring prompting the actions of these birds, is so powerful as to remind us of the disease called *nostalgia*, or *mal du pays*, or *home-sickness*, which sometimes attacks human beings when long deprived of the comforts of home. This disease is oftenest observed among the natives of mountainous countries, but is not confined to them. It has been observed in Swiss, French, and Scotch soldiers, when on long-protracted foreign service, and is always aggravated by the music of their native land. Thus the Swiss pastoral air of the " Ranz des Vaches," will produce or increase the home-sickness of the Swiss soldiery, when there is no prospect of a return home, and the sound of bag-pipes will have a similar effect on the Scottish troops. Men are more liable to it than women, from being oftener called from their homes; but cases have occurred among female servants, who have gone to places at a great distance from home.

The disease begins by great dejection of spirits, with a desire to conceal the cause. The patient soon becomes nervous and emaciated in a high degree. His sleep is disturbed and feverish, and an oppressive lethargy is upon him by day. If relief be not speedily obtained, some fatal disease soon sets in, or those already existing are rendered mortal. Medicine has very little power over this disease, and reasoning with the patient is of little avail, unless it is possible to hold out the hope of a return home. If this can be done, the effect is speedy and wonderful. A person who appears to be at the point of death will often revive, and rapidly recover strength and spirits under the assured hope of going home. There is no other effectual remedy for the complaint when it has once set in. The most effectual preventives of home-sickness are kind treatment and abundant employment. On long and tedious voyages there is danger of sailors' becoming affected by it, and therefore, the commanders of vessels are anxious, in such circumstances, to find occupation and amusement for their crews. The worst cases of this disease are always seen in regiments where the officers are harsh and severe, and among servants whose masters are cruel and tyrannical.

The home-sickness of the dove is scarcely to be considered as a disease, for the bird endures captivity tolerably well; but its powerful effect in urging the bird to immediate return, at whatever distance it may regain its liberty, is a strong point of resemblance to the malady just described.

Some of the most remarkable journeys performed by pigeons, as it respects the rapidity of flight, and the numbers in motion at the same time, are those of the passenger-pigeons of America, whose history has been given by the eminent naturalists, Wilson and Audubon, and therefore cannot be doubted, although on less respectable authority it would appear past belief. As an instance of their rapid flight, it is stated, that passenger-pigeons have been killed in the neighborhood of New-York with their crops full of rice, which they must have collected in the fields of Georgia and Carolina, these districts being the nearest in which they could possibly have procured a supply of this kind of food. As their power of digestion is so great that they will decompose food entirely in twelve hours, they must in this case have travelled between three and four hundred miles in six hours, which gives an average speed of a mile a minute. The power of vision is also great in these birds, for, while travelling at that swift rate, they inspect the country below, and on discovering a spot where food is plentiful, they alight on it in countless multitudes. To give some idea of the amount of pigeons which migrate at certain seasons, from place to place, in America, we give the following relation, in the words of Audubon :

"In the Autumn of 1813, I left my house at Henderson, on the banks of the Ohio, on my way to Louisville. In passing over the Barrens, a few miles beyond Hardensburgh, I observed the pigeons flying from north-east to 'south-west in greater numbers than I thought I had ever seen them before ; and feeling an inclination to count the flocks that might pass within the reach of my eye in one hour, I dismounted, seated myself on an eminence, and began to mark with my pencil, making a dot for every flock that passed. In a short time, finding the task I had undertaken impracticable, as the birds poured in in countless multitudes, I rose, and counting the dots then put down, found that one hundred and sixty-three had been made in twenty-one minutes. I travelled on, and still met more the farther I proceeded. The air was literally filled with pigeons, and the continued buzz of wings had a tendency to lull me to repose. Before sunset I reached Louisville, distant from Hardensburgh fifty-five miles; the pigeons were still passing in undiminished numbers, and continued to do so for two or three days in succession. The people were all in arms. The banks of the Ohio were crowded with men and boys, incessantly shooting at the pilgrims, which then flew lower as they passed the river. Multitudes were destroyed. For a week or more the population fed on no other flesh than that of pigeons, and talked of nothing but pigeons."

These migrations are performed in search of food ; and where beech-mast is abundant, the flocks wheel round and alight, filling the woods with their numbers. Thus they feed till the middle of the day, when they settle on the branches and rest till sunset. At that time they rise *en masse*, and depart to some general roosting-place, whither all the flocks, for hundreds of miles, appear to resort. This roosting-place is always in a forest where the trees are of great size, and where there is little underwood. The enormous flights of pigeons arriving there after sunset, and the manner in which they congregate in dense masses, form a most astonishing spectacle. Audubon rode through a portion of the forest, forty miles in extent, and three in breadth, chosen by these birds as a roosting-place. It was on the banks of the Green River, in Kentucky, and was frequently visited by the naturalist. He says, " My first view of it was about a fortnight subsequent to the period when they made choice of it, and I arrived there nearly two hours before sunset. Few pigeons were then to be seen, but a great number of persons with horses and wagons, guns and ammunition, had already established encampments on the borders. Two farmers, from the vicinity of Russelsville, distant more than a hundred miles, had driven upwards of three hundred hogs to be fattened on the pigeons that were to be slaughtered. Here and there people employed in plucking and salting what had already been procured, were seen sitting in the midst of large piles of these birds. Many trees, two feet in diameter, I observed were broken off at no great distance from the ground; and the branches of many of the largest and tallest had given way, as if the forest had been swept by a tornado. Everything proved to me that the number of birds resorting to this part of the forest must be immense beyond conception. As the period of their arrival approached, their foes anxiously prepared to receive them; some were furnished with iron pots containing sulphur; others with torches of pine-knots; many with poles, and the rest with guns. The sun was lost to our view, yet not a pigeon had arrived. Everything was ready, and all eyes were gazing on the clear sky, which appeared in glimpses amidst the tall trees. Suddenly there burst forth a general cry of 'Here they come!' The noise which they made, though yet distant, reminded me of a hard gale at sea, passing through the rigging of a close-reefed vessel. As the birds arrived, and passed over me, I felt a current of air that surprised me. Thousands were soon knocked down by the polemen; the birds continued to pour in; the fires were lighted, and a most magnificent as well as wonderful and almost terrifying sight presented itself.— The pigeons arriving by thousands, alighted everywhere, one above another, until solid masses as large as hogsheads were found on the branches all round.— Here and there the perches gave way with a crash, and falling on the ground, destroyed hundreds of the birds beneath, forcing down the dense groups with which every stick was loaded. It was a scene of uproar and confusion; no one dared venture within the line of devastation: the hogs had been penned up in due time, the picking up of the dead and wounded being left for the next morning's employment. The pigeons were constantly coming, and it was past midnight before I perceived a decrease in the number of those that arrived. Towards the approach of day, the noise in some measure subsided ; long before objects were distinguishable, the pigeons began to move off in a direction quite different from that in which they had arrived the evening before, and at sunrise, all that were able to fly had disappeared. The howling of the wolves now reached our ears, and the foxes, lynxes, cougars, bears, raccoons, and opossums, were seen sneaking off, while eagles and hawks of different species, accompanied by a crowd of vultures, came to supplant them, and enjoy their share of the spoil."

Either a roosting-place or a breeding-place of these birds is looked upon by the Indians as their grand dependence and a

general source of profit for the season.—
The plumage of the passenger-pigeon is
blue on the head and neck, and greyish
on the back, wings, and tail. The under
parts are brownish red, with rich reflections of gold, emerald, and crimson. The
length of the bird is sixteen inches and a
half. The female is duller in plumage,
and of rather smaller size. Passenger-
pigeons, notwithstanding their migratory
nature and powerful flight, can be recon-
ciled to the confinement of an aviary, and
become very tame.

We have already noticed the plaintive
notes of doves. These are not, however,
the sounds of lamentations, but those of
tenderness and love. The cooing of the
Zenaida dove is said to be peculiarly
touching, so that one who hears it for the
first time, naturally stops to ask, " What
bird is that ?" Its effect on the feelings

is illustrated by an anecdote respecting a pirate, who was associated with a band of the most desperate villains that ever annoyed the navigation of the Florida coast. This man had frequent occasion to repair to certain wells, near which the doves nestled, and their soft and melancholy cry was the means of awakening in his breast feelings which had long slumbered, and of melting his heart to repentance. He was accustomed to linger at the spot, and to contrast his guilty and wretched life with former days of comparative innocence and peace. He said that he never left the wells without increased fears and misgivings respecting futurity, and at last he became so deeply moved by these notes, the only soothing sounds he ever heard during his life of horrors, that he poured out his soul in supplications for mercy, and firmly resolved to abandon his desperate companions, and mode of life, and to return to his own family, who were deploring his absence. His escape from his vessel was accompanied by many difficulties and dangers, but no danger seemed to him comparable to that of living in the violation of human and divine laws. At last he happily reached his former home, and settled in peace among his friends. Thus were the notes of this gentle bird employed as a means of penetrating the sinner's heart, and reclaiming him from the error of his ways; and thus may the feeblest instruments be made effectual to accomplish mighty ends.

Audubon, speaking of the Zenaida dove of the West India Islands, says, that when sitting on her eggs, or when her young are still small, she rarely removes from them, unless an attempt be made to catch her, which she, however, evades with great dexterity. "On several occasions of this kind, I have thought that the next moment would render me the possessor of 'one of' these doves alive. Her beautiful eye was steadily bent on mine, in which she must have discovered my intention; her body was gently made to retire sideways to the farther edge of her nest as my hand drew nearer to her, and just as I thought I had hold of her, off she glided with the quickness of thought, taking to wing at once. She would then alight within a few yards of me, and watch my motions with so much sorrow, that her wings drooped, and her whole frame trembled as if suffering from intense cold. Who could stand such a scene of despair? I left the mother to her eggs or offspring." The powerful instinct which could subdue the natural timidity of the dove, and induce her to sit quietly on her eggs, in the presence of danger, reminds us of some remarks on this subject from the pen of a very pleasing writer, the author of the Journal of a Naturalist.

" The extraordinary change of character which many creatures exhibit, from timidity to boldness and rage, from stupidity to art and stratagem, for the preservation of a helpless offspring, seems to be an established ordination of Providence, actuating in various degrees most of the races of animated beings; and we have few examples of this influencing principle more obvious than that of the missel thrush,, in which a creature addicted to solitude and shyness will abandon its haunts, and associate with those it fears, to preserve its offspring from an enemy more merciless and predaceous still. The love of offspring, one of the strongest impressions given to created beings, and inseparable

from their nature, is ordained by the
Almighty as the means of preservation
under helplessness and want. Dependent, totally dependent as is the creature,
for everything that can contribute to exist-
ence and support, upon the Great Creator
of all things, so are new-born feebleness
and blindness dependent upon the parent
that produced them; and to the latter is
given intensity of love, to overbalance the
privations and sufferings required from it.
This love, that changes the nature of the
timid and gentle to boldness and fury, ex-
poses the parent to injury and death, from
which its wiles and cautions do not always secure it; and in man, the avarice
of possession will at times subdue his
merciful and better feelings. Beautifully
imbued with celestial justice and human-
ity, as all the ordinations which the Isra-
elites received in the wilderness were,

there is nothing more impressive, nothing more accordant with the divinity of our nature, than the particular injunctions which were given in respect to showing mercy to the maternal creature cherishing its young, when by reason of its parental regard it might be placed in danger.— The eggs, the offspring, were allowed to be taken; but 'thou shalt in anywise let the dam go;' 'thou shalt not, in one day, kill both an ewe and her young.' 'The ardent affection, the tenderness with which I have filled the parent, is in no way to lead to its injury or destruction:' and this is enforced not by command only, not by the threat of punishment and privation, but by the assurance of temporal reward, by promise of the greatest blessings that can be found on earth, length of days and prosperity."

The notes of the ground-dove are described by Audubon as being peculiarly touching when heard in the calm of a 'spring morn among the islands which protect the shores of South Carolina, Georgia, and the Floridas, " where the air is rendered balmy by the effluvia of thousands of flowers, each of which rivals its neighbour in the brilliancy of its hues. Stop there, kind reader, and seat yourself beneath the broadly extended arms of the thickly-leaved ever-green oak, and at that joyous moment when the first beams of the sun reach your eye, see the owl passing low and swiftly over the ground in haste to reach his diurnal retreat before the increasing light renders all things dim to his sight ; observe the leathern-winged bat pursuing his undulating course through the dewy air, now reflecting downwards to seize the retiring nocturnal insect, now upwards to pursue another species, as it rises to meet the genial warmth emitted by the orb of day. Listen—for at such a moment your soul will be touched by sounds—to the soft, the mellow, the melting accents, which we might suppose inspired by Nature's self, and which she has taught the ground-dove to employ in conveying the expression of his love to his mate, who is listening to them with delight."

Ground-doves find their food chiefly on the ground, and have their flying feathers less developed than the other kinds of pigeon. They flit from place to place, but always alight at short distances.— There are numerous species of these birds. The American ground-dove is abundant in the southern states of America, and in the West India islands, where the French planters call it the ortolan. It feeds on rice, seeds, and berries, and is oftener met with in open fields and plantations than in forests. It is a slender and delicate bird, little capable of enduring severe weather, from which it retreats southwards, as soon as winter sets in. This ground-dove is little more than six inches long; the breast, throat, and sides of the neck are of a pale wine-coloured purple; the crown and back of the head are of a rich pale blue, mixed with purple. The wing feathers are dusky on the outsides, but of a rich red chestnut beneath, the tail is brown and black, tipped with white. This beautiful bird is sometimes kept in cages in the West Indies, where its plaintive note is much esteemed.

The copper-coloured ground-dove is another species inhabiting the same countries, but feeding on elevated and rocky mountains. It runs along the ground in the manner of a partridge, and is known

in Jamaica as " the mountain partridge ;"
but it always perches on a bush, or low
branch of a tree when it reposes. It forms
its nest upon the ground, in some sheltered
spot, and lays two eggs. The whole of
the upper plumage of this bird, including
that of the head and neck, is bright
orange, glossed with rich purple, which
gives it the coppery appearance denoted
by its name. Another beautiful dove of
the West India islands is the blue-headed
ground dove. The general plumage is
deep brown, with a shade of purple, and
the head is of a rich azure blue. There
are many other ground-doves, having rich
and beautiful plumage, as well as a plaintive cry.

Another species of dove equally celebrated with the ground-dove for the melancholy and affecting sound of its notes,
and also esteemed on account of the deli-

cate flavour of its flesh, is the Carolina turtle, a North American bird, which wanders as far as Canada in summer, but appears to make the Carolinas its principal winter quarters.   Wilson says, that those who wander in the American woods in the spring, will there hear many a singular and sprightly performer, but none so mournful as the Carolina turtle.   " The hopeless wo of settled sorrow, swelling the heart of female innocence itself, could not assume tones more sad, more tender, or affecting.   Its notes are four; the first is somewhat the highest and preparatory, seeming to be uttered with an inspiration of the breath, as if the afflicted creature were just recovering its voice from the last convulsive sobs of distress; this is followed by three long, deep, and mournful moanings, that no person of sensibility can listen to without sympathy; a pause of a few minutes ensues, and again the solemn voice of sorrow is renewed as before.— This is usually heard in the deepest parts of the woods, frequently about noon and towards evening." With music so exquisitely sad, it must be difficult to realize the fact, that the bird is giving utterance to feelings of delight, and is cheering his mate as she sits on her nest.

As soon as frost sets in, these birds begin their migration to the south, and in winter the woods of Carolina and Georgia swarm with them, so that the rustling of their wings is heard in all quarters. It is at this time that they become an easy prey to the fowler, and are in the best condition for his purpose. They move northward in March, or early in April, but not in large flocks. On the contrary, they are commonly much scattered, flying in pairs, alighting in farm-yards, and mixing

familiarly with common poultry, especially
at feeding time.   Their flight is swift and
vigorous, and always accompanied with
a whistling of the wings, by which they
are easily known from the carrier-pigeon.
They alight on trees, fences, or on the
ground, and are exceedingly fond of buck-
wheat, hemp-seed, and Indian corn.—
They devour large quantities of gravel,
and frequently visit gardens for the sake
of the peas, of which they are particularly
greedy.   These birds are very beautiful
in their plumage.   The crown, upper part
of the neck, and wings, are of a fine silky
slate-blue ; the back is ashy brown, the
sides of the neck and breast pale orange-
brown: under the ear feathers is a spot
or drop of deep black, immediately below
which the plumage reflects the most vivid
tints of green, gold, and crimson.   The legs
and feet are coral-red, seamed with white.

The eyes are of a glossy blackness, surrounded with a pale greenish blue skin.

In Southern Africa there is a very curious and beautiful little pigeon, scarcely weighing more than a common sparrow. It is called the cape-turtle, and is very generally distributed over Africa, south of the desert, and even down to the valley of the Nile, as far as Nubia. This little bird is only seven inches long, and more than the half of that is occupied by the tail. The plumage of the head, sides of the neck and smaller coverts of the wings, are pale French grey, passing into a brown grey on the back. A remarkable patch of deep black passes over the forehead, the sides of the head as far as the eyes, the chin, throat and fore sides of the neck and breast, where it is prettily rounded off. Black or purplish spots and bands also ornament the wings and tail, and exhibit metallic reflections. Very little is known of the habits of this beautiful bird, farther than that it follows the general law of the other turtles by nestling in trees, and seeking its food upon the ground. The eggs are two in number, white and nearly transparent, and so delicate that they can scarcely be touched without being broken.

People are apt to suppose that the eggs of birds are all very much alike ; so much so, that when a striking resemblance between two different objects is required, it is commonly said that they are as much alike as two eggs. Now the fact is, that the wonderful variety which is every where found among the productions of nature is also observed among the eggs of birds. Mr. Hewitson, in his beautiful work on the *Eggs of British Birds*, has given accurately colored engravings of several hundred eggs, and it is impossible to examine them without being struck with the remarkable variety in the colour, size, and even form of eggs. As an example of their great difference in colour and form, we give the figures of the eggs of the Ring Dove, the Turtle Dove, and the Ringed Plover, which is also called

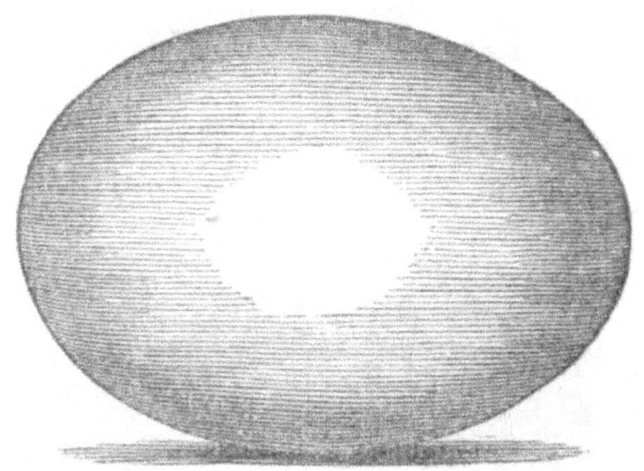

EGG OF THE RING DOVE.

the Ring Dotterel or Sand Lark. "This bird," says Mr. Hewitson, "breeds in most parts of our sea-coast, being most frequent near the mouths of rivers and smaller streams: it makes no nest, but

lays its four *conical* eggs in a slight hole
on the surface of the ground, either
amongst small gravel or upon the little
hillocks of sand which occur so com-

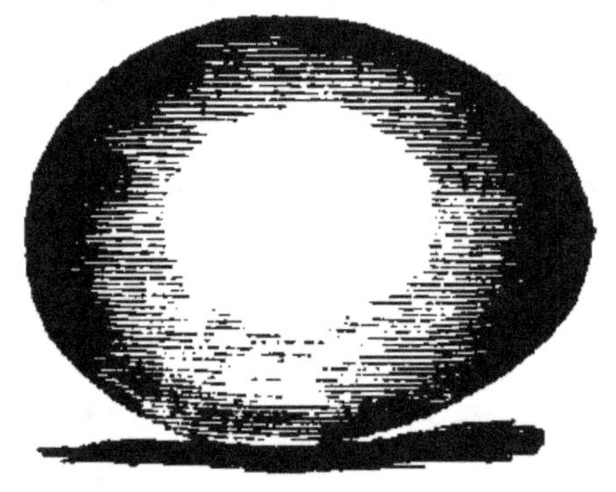

EGG OF THE TURTLE DOVE.

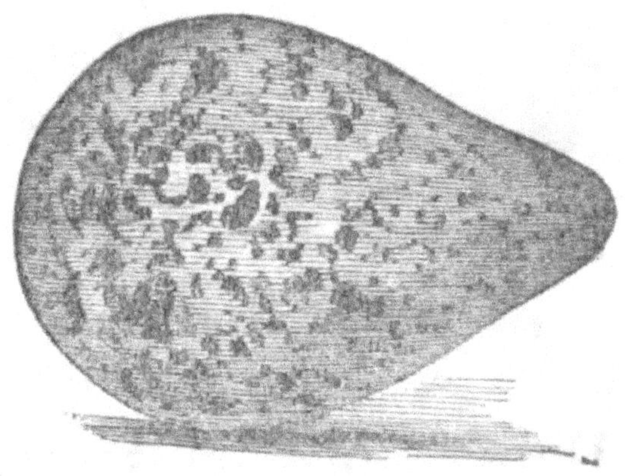

EGG OF THE RINGED PLOVER.

monly on our flat beach. In some I
have seen the eggs present a very beautiful appearance upon the clean white

sand, frequently near the root of some
tall grasses which wave over them as a
protection against the storm. These ac-
tive little birds are ever on the watch,
and moving long ere you reach their
eggs, making little circuits round you,
and uttering their sweet, plaintive whistle,
by which you may always infer the near
neighbourhood of their eggs or young."

THE TURTLE DOVE.

When good Nathanael's praise I read,
  In Scripture's page renown'd,
"Behold an Israelite indeed,
  In whom no guile is found;'

Methinks his fame is higher far
  Than kings or heroes gain,
Who reap their laurels in the war
  But not without a stain.

The gentle words that banish strife
  Our common joys increase;
But what is home, and what is life,
  Without the bond of peace?

Then would'st thou earn thy Saviour's praise,
  Whose eye regards the young;
Let meek discretion guide thy ways,
  And kindness rule thy tongue.

So shalt thou learn to keep in sight
  The wisdom from above;
With circumspection to unite
  The mildness of the Dove.

Sweet bird! her guileless ways I know;
  Then let me learn from thence,
To study peace where'er I go,
  And never give offence.

Do thou, blest Spirit, source of peace,
  Thy heav'nly grace impart;
Bid every angry passion cease
  And sanctify my heart.